Christmas Orna to Crochet

Barbara Christopher

Dover Publications, Inc.
Mineola, New York

Copyright

Copyright © 1993, 1995, 2014 by Dover Publications, Inc.
All rights reserved.

Bibliographical Note

Christmas Ornaments to Crochet, first published by Dover Publications, Inc., in 2014, contains a selection of projects from the following previously published Dover books by Barbara Christopher: *Elegant Christmas Ornaments to Crochet* (1995) and *Victorian Crocheted Christmas Ornaments* (1993).

International Standard Book Number

ISBN-13: 978-0-486-78961-3
ISBN-10: 0-486-78961-6

Manufactured in the United States by LSC Communications
78961603   2018
www.doverpublications.com

Introduction

Christmas is a time for decorating—windows, trees, packages, cards, tables, and anything else you can think of. Nothing makes a more elegant Christmas decoration than a crisp, dainty, crocheted snowflake, star, or other ornament. Here are more than 50 different ornaments to choose from.

The ornaments are made with three different sizes of DMC* Cebelia—#10, 20, and 30. You can easily change the size of the ornament by using a different size thread and hook. The ornaments look best if they are crocheted tightly, so you may find that you need to use a smaller or larger hook than called for in the instructions in order to get the effect you want.

Each ornament should be blocked and starched to give it a crisp look. If the piece is soiled, wash it in warm water with a mild soap. Rinse it thoroughly and roll it in a towel to remove the excess moisture.

Commercial products are available to stiffen the ornaments, but "homemade" solutions work just as well. The traditional (but messy) choice is sugar starch. To make it, mix equal amounts of sugar and water in a small pan. Bring the mixture to a rapid boil, then let it cool to room temperature. Another possibility is to use white craft glue diluted with an equal amount of water. I usually use a thick solution of commercial boilable starch. Don't use a spray or liquid starch; they won't give the piece enough body.

Fill a bowl with the stiffening solution and immerse the crocheted piece for several minutes. Take it out and gently press out the excess solution—the piece should still be very wet. Place the piece right side up on a plastic-covered pinning board (I use a piece of pressed cardboard). Using rustproof pins, carefully pin the piece to shape, starting at the center and pinning each point and picot in place. For the Layered Star on page 22, shape the upper points while the star is still slightly damp. To make blocking the ornaments easier, I have included several guides (see page 55)—one for 6- or 12-pointed snowflakes**, one for 5-pointed stars, one for 7-pointed ornaments and one for 9- or 18-pointed ornaments. Trace the appropriate guide onto tissue or tracing paper and extend the arms out to the finished size of the piece. Place the guide under the plastic on the pinning board. As you pin, align the points with the arms of the guide. For wreaths and circles, draw a circle of the appropriate size. Let the piece dry thoroughly before removing the pins.

---

*For information on where to obtain DMC threads, write to the DMC Corporation, 10 Basin Drive, Suite 130, Kearny, NJ 07032.

**Used with the permission of the American School of Needlework, Inc., ASN Publishing, 1455 Linda Vista Drive, San Marcos, CA 92069.

Lace Circle Star

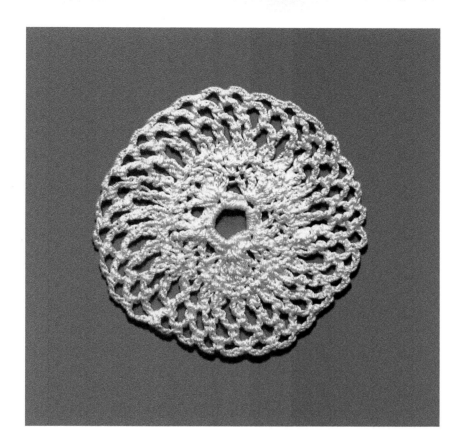

Approximately 2¾" in diameter

Materials:

DMC Cebelia #20, 11 yds.
Size 10 steel crochet hook

Ch 12; join with sl st in first ch to form ring.

Rnd 1: Ch 1, (4 sc in ring, ch 2) 5 times; join with sl st in first sc of rnd.

Rnd 2: Ch 1, turn, sl st in ch-2 sp, turn; ch 3 (counts as dc), in same sp, work dc, tr, 2 dtr, tr and dc, (in next ch-2 sp, work dc, tr, 2 dtr, tr and dc) 4 times; sl st in top of beg ch 3.

Rnd 3: Ch 1, sc in same sp, *ch 6, sl st in 6th ch from hook for picot,* *sc in next st, work p, rep from * around; sl st in first sc of rnd.

Rnd 4: Work sl st and ch 1 up side of p to top, ch 1, sc in same p, ch 4, (sc in next p, ch 4) 29 times; ch 2, hdc in first sc of rnd (this brings thread into position for next rnd).

Rnd 5: Ch 1, sc around post of st just made, ch 4, (sc in next ch-4 lp, ch 4) 29 times, ch 2, hdc in first sc of rnd.

Rnd 6: Ch 1, sc around post of st just made, ch 3, *sc in next ch-4 lp, ch 3, rep from * around; sl st in first sc of rnd. Fasten off.

Picot Heart

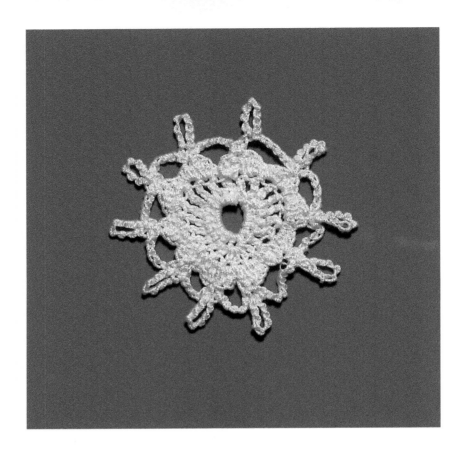

Approximately 1¾" in diameter

Materials:

DMC Cebelia #30, 6 yds.
Size 12 steel crochet hook

Ch 11; join with sl st in first ch to form ring.

Rnd 1: Ch 1, 16 sc in ring; sl st in first sc of rnd.

Rnd 2: Ch 3 (counts as dc), dc in next sc, tr in next sc, 2 dtr in next sc, dtr in next sc, (tr in next sc) twice, dc in next sc, 5 dc in next sc for bottom point, dc in next sc, (tr in next sc) twice, dtr in next sc, 2 dtr in next sc, tr in next sc, dc in next sc; sl st in top of beg ch 3.

Rnd 3: Ch 1, (sc, hdc and dc in next st, dc, hdc and sc in next st) 11 times; sl st in first sc of rnd.

Rnd 4: Sl st to sp bet first 2 dc, ch 1, (sc in same sp, *ch 9, sl st in 9th ch from hook for picot*, sc in same sp, ch 5, (work sc, p, sc and ch 5 bet the dc of next point) 10 times; sl st in first sc of rnd. Fasten off.

Glittering Snowflake

Approximately 2" in diameter

Materials:

DMC Cebelia #30, 5 yds.
Size 12 steel crochet hook

Ch 12; join with sl st in first ch to form ring.

Rnd 1: Ch 1, 18 sc in ring; sl st in first sc of rnd.

Rnd 2: Ch 1, sc in same sp, work hdc, dc and hdc in next sc, sc in next sc, (sc in next sc, work hdc, dc and hdc in next sc, sc in next sc) 5 times; sl st in first sc of rnd.

Rnd 3: Sl st in next hdc and dc, ch 1, sc in same sp, ch 6, (skip 4 sts, sc in next dc, ch 6) 5 times, skip 4 sts; sl st in first sc of rnd.

Rnd 4: Ch 8 (counts as dc and ch 5), (*dc in next ch-6 sp, ch 5,* dc in next sc, ch 5) 5 times, rep bet *s once; sl st in 3rd ch of beg ch 8.

Rnd 5: Ch 1, (work 2 sc, hdc, dc and tr in next ch-5 sp, *ch 6, sl st in 6th ch from hook for picot,* work tr, dc, hdc and 2 sc in next ch-5 sp) 6 times; sl st in first sc of rnd. Fasten off.

Bow

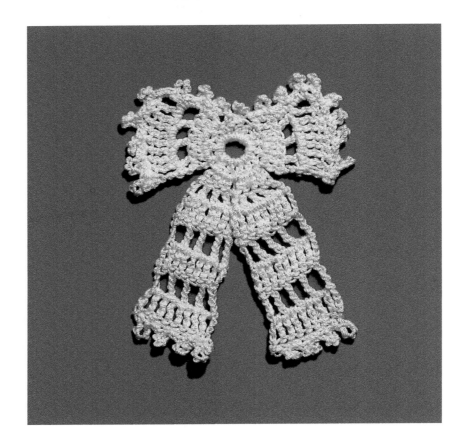

Approximately 2½" by 3½"

Materials:

DMC Cebelia #20, 13 yds.
Size 10 steel crochet hook

Ch 9; join with sl st in first ch to form ring.

Center Ring: Ch 3 (counts as first dc), 13 dc in ring; sl st in top of beg ch 3.

Loops—Row 1: Ch 3 (counts as first dc), dc in same dc, (2 dc in next dc) 3 times—8 dc.

Row 2: Ch 5, turn (counts as dc and ch 2), skip next dc, (dc in next dc, ch 2, skip next dc) 2 times, dc in next dc, dc in top of turning ch 3.

Row 3: Ch 4, turn (counts as tr), (tr in next dc, 2 tr in next ch-2 sp) 3 times, tr in 3rd ch of beg ch 5. Fasten off. With same side facing, skip 4 sc on center ring; attach thread in next sc. Rep rows 1–3.

Row 4: Ch 1, turn, sc in first tr, (*ch 6, sl st in 6th ch from hook for picot,* sc in next 2 tr) 4 times, work p, sc in next tr and in top of turning ch, work p, 2 sc around turning ch, work p, (2 sc in end of next row, work p) 2 times, sc in each of next 2 sc of center ring, work p, (2 sc in end of next row, work p) 3 times, sc in each of next 2 tr, work p, (sc in next 2 tr, work p) 4 times, sc in last tr. Fasten off.

Streamers: With right side facing, attach thread in first free sc of center ring.

(continued on the next page)

Row 1: Ch 3, 2 dc in same sp, 2 dc in next sp.

Row 2: Ch 4, turn (counts as dc and ch 1), (dc in next dc, ch 1) 3 times, dc in 3rd ch of turning ch.

Row 3: Ch 4, turn (counts as tr), (tr in next ch-1 sp, tr in next dc) 3 times, tr in next ch-1 sp, tr in top of turning ch.

Row 4: Ch 5, turn (counts as tr and ch 1), skip next tr, (tr in next tr, ch 1, skip next tr) 3 times, tr in 4th ch of turning ch.

Rows 5 & 6: Repeat rows 3 & 4.

Row 7: Repeat row 3.

Row 8: Ch 1, turn, sc in first tr, work p, (sc in each of next 2 tr, work p) 3 times; sc in next tr. Fasten off. With right side facing, attach thread in next free sc on center ring, repeat rows 1–8 of streamers.

Wagon Wheel Ornament

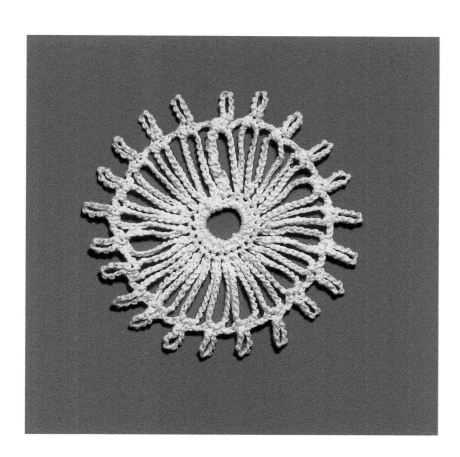

Approximately 3" in diameter

Materials:

DMC Cebelia #20, 8 yds.
Size 10 steel crochet hook

Ch 14; join with sl st in first ch to form ring.

Rnd 1: Ch 2 (counts as hdc), 21 hdc in ring; sl st in top of beg ch 2.

Rnd 2: Ch 1, sc in same sp, ch 20, (sc in next hdc, ch 20) 21 times; sl st in first sc of rnd.

Rnd 3: Work sl st and ch 1 up side of first ch-20 lp to top, ch 1, sc in same lp, *ch 9, sl st in 9th ch from hook for picot,* sc in same lp, ch 2, (sc in next ch-20 lp, work p, sc in same lp, ch 2) 21 times; sl st in first sc of rnd. Fasten off.

Open Star

Approximately 3" in diameter

Materials:

DMC Cebelia #20, 11 yds.
Size 10 steel crochet hook

Ch 10; join with sl st in first ch to form ring.

Rnd 1: Ch 1, 20 sc in ring; sl st in first sc of rnd.

Rnd 2: Ch 1, sc in same sp, (ch 20, skip 3 sc, sc in next sc) 4 times, ch 20, skip 3 sc; sl st in first sc of rnd. Fasten off.

Rnd 3: Join thread to top of any ch-20 lp, ch 1, sc in same lp, ch 6, sc in same lp, ch 9, (sc in next lp, ch 6, sc in same lp, ch 9) 4 times; join in first sc of rnd.

Rnd 4: Ch 1 *in next ch-6 lp, work (2 sc, *ch 6, sl st in 6th ch from hook for picot*) twice, 2 sc in same lp, in next ch-9 lp, work (2 sc, p) 4 times, 2 sc in same lp; rep from * around; sl st in first sc of rnd. Fasten off.

Rnd 5: Join thread to top of any p, ch 1, sc in p, work p, sc in same p, ch 2, *sc in next p, work p, sc in same p, ch 2; rep from * around; sl st in first sc of rnd. Fasten off.

Picot Wreath

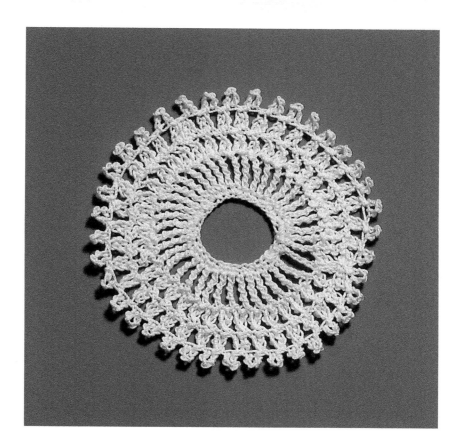

Approximately 3¼" in diameter

Materials:

DMC Cebelia #20, 16 yds.
Size 10 steel crochet hook

Ch 30; join with sl st in first ch to form ring, being careful not to twist chain.

Rnd 1: Ch 1, sc in same sp and in next ch, 2 sc in next ch, (sc in each of next 2 ch, 2 sc in next ch) 9 times; join in first sc of rnd—40 sc.

Rnd 2: Ch 5 (counts as dtr), *ch 6, sl st in 6th ch from hook to form picot*, *dtr in next sc, work picot as before; rep from * around; join in top of beg ch 5.

Rnd 3: Sl st to top of first p, ch 1, sc in same p, work p, *sc in next p, work p; rep from * around; sl st in first sc of rnd.

Rnd 4: Sl st to top of first p, work p, *sl st in next p, work p; rep from * around, sl st in first sl st. Fasten off.

Scalloped Snowflake

Approximately 3½" in diameter

Materials:

DMC Cebelia #20, 15 yds.
Size 10 steel crochet hook

Ch 10; join with sl st in first ch to form ring.

Rnd 1: Ch 1, 18 sc in ring; sl st in first sc of rnd.

Rnd 2: Ch 4 (counts as tr), tr in each of next 2 sc, (ch 7, tr in each of next 3 sc) 5 times, ch 3, tr in top of beg ch 4 (this brings thread into position for next rnd).

Rnd 3: Ch 1, sc around post of tr just made, ch 12, (sc in 4th ch of next ch 7 sp, ch 12) 5 times; sl st in first sc of rnd.

Rnd 4: Ch 1, sc in same sp, (*in ch-12 sp, work 2 sc, 2 hdc, 2 dc, 2 tr, 2 dc, 2 hdc, 2 sc,* sc in next sc) 5 times; rep bet *s once; sl st in first sc of rnd.

Rnd 5: Ch 5 (counts as dc and ch 2), *skip 1 st, dc in next st, ch 2; rep from * around; sl st in 3rd ch of beg ch 5.

Rnd 6: Ch 1, *sc in next ch-2 sp, *ch 6, sl st in 6th ch from hook for picot*; rep from * around; sl st in first sc of rnd. Fasten off.

9-Pointed Ornament

Approximately 2½" in diameter

Materials:

DMC Cebelia #30, 7 yds.
Size 12 steel crochet hook

Ch 9; join with sl st in first ch to form ring.

Rnd 1: Ch 2 (counts as hdc), 17 hdc in ring; sl st in top of beg ch 2.

Rnd 2: Ch 3 (counts as dc), dc in same sp, ch 2, (skip next hdc, 2 dc in next hdc, ch 2) 8 times; sl st in top of beg ch 3.

Rnd 3: Sl st in next dc and in ch-2 sp, ch 3 (counts as dc), 2 dc in same ch-2 sp, (*ch 3, sl st bet next 2 hdc, *ch 6, sl st in 6th ch from hook for picot, sl st bet same 2 hdc, ch 3,* 3 dc in next ch-2 sp) 8 times; rep bet *s once; sl st in top of beg ch 3.

Rnd 4: Ch 1, sc in next dc, (ch 9, sc in center dc of next group) 8 times; ch 4, dtr in first sc of rnd (this brings thread into position for next rnd).

Rnd 5: Ch 1, sc around post of dtr just made, (*ch 9, sl st in 9th ch from hook for large picot,* sc in same sp as last sc, ch 9,* sc in next ch-9 sp) 8 times; rep bet *s once; sl st in first sc of rnd. Fasten off.

Sunlight Ornament

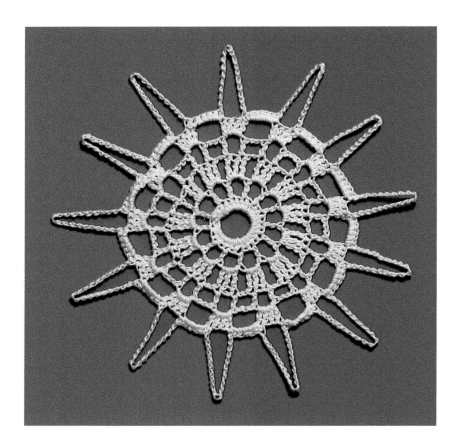

Approximately 4½" in diameter

Materials:

DMC Cebelia #20, 14 yds.
Size 10 steel crochet hook

Ch 15; join with sl st in first ch to form ring.

Rnd 1: Ch 2 (counts as hdc), 25 hdc in ring; sl st in top of beg ch 2.

Rnd 2: Ch 6 (counts as dc and ch 3), (skip next hdc, dc in next hdc, ch 3) 12 times, skip next dc; sl st in 3rd ch of beg ch 6.

Rnd 3: Sl st in first ch-3 sp, ch 4, 2 tr in same ch-3 sp, ch 2, *3 tr in next ch-3 sp, ch 2; rep from * around; sl st in top of beg ch 4.

Rnd 4: Ch 6 (counts as dc and ch 3), skip next tr, dc in next tr, ch 3, skip next ch-2 sp, *dc in next tr, ch 3, skip next tr, dc in next tr, ch 3, skip next ch-2 sp; rep from * around; sl st in 3rd ch of beg ch 6.

Rnd 5: Sl st in next ch-sp, ch 3 (counts as dc), 3 dc in same sp, ch 5, *skip next ch-3 sp, 4 dc in next ch-3 sp, ch 5; rep from * around, skip next ch-3 sp; sl st in top of beg ch 3.

Rnd 6: Ch 1, sc in same sp, *ch 20, skip 2 dc, sc in next dc, 5 sc in next ch-5 sp,** sc in next sc; rep from *, ending last rep at **; sl st in first sc of rnd. Fasten off.

Airy Snowflake

Approximately 3½" in diameter

Materials:

DMC Cebelia #30, 9 yds.
Size 12 steel crochet hook

Ch 12; join with sl st in first ch to form ring, being careful not to twist chain.

Rnd 1: Ch 1, sc in same ch, ch 6, (sc in next ch, ch 6) 10 times, ch 3, dc in first sc of rnd (this brings thread into position for next rnd).

Rnd 2: Ch 1, sc around post of dc just made, (*ch 3, *ch 6, sl st in 6th ch from hook for picot, ch 3, sc in next ch-6 lp,* ch 6, sc in next ch-6 lp) 5 times; rep bet *s once; ch 3, dc in first sc of rnd.

Rnd 3: Ch 1, sc around post of dc just made, *(ch 3, work p) 3 times, ch 3, skip next picot-lp,*

sc in next ch-6 lp) 5 times; rep bet *s once; sl st in first sc of rnd.

Rnd 4: Sl st in each of next 3 chs, work sl st and ch 1 to top of first p, ch 1, sc in same p, (*ch 6, work p, ch 6, skip next p, sc in next p, ch 3, work p, ch 3*, sc in next p) 5 times; rep bet *s once; sl st in first sc of rnd.

Rnd 5: Ch 1, sc in same sp, (*ch 9, work p, ch 9, sc in next sc, ch 5, work p, ch 5*, sc in next sc) 5 times; rep bet *s once; sl st in first sc of rnd. Fasten off.

7-Pointed Star

Approximately 2" in diameter

Materials:

DMC Cebelia #30, 5 yds.
Size 12 steel crochet hook

Ch 12; join with sl st in first ch to form ring.

Rnd 1: Ch 1, 21 sc in ring; sl st in first sc of rnd.

Rnd 2: Ch 1, sc in same sp and in each of next 2 sc, *ch 6, sl st in 6th ch from hook for picot,* sc in last sc worked in, (sc in each of next 3 sc, work p, sc in last sc worked in) 6 times; sl st in first sc of rnd.

Rnd 3: Ch 1, (sc in next sc, ch 9, skip next sc, p and next 2 sc) 7 times; sl st in first sc of rnd.

Rnd 4: Ch 1, sc in same sp, ch 12, (sc in next sc, ch 12) 6 times; sl st in first sc of rnd.

Rnd 5: Ch 1, sc in same sp, (*ch 7, sl st in center ch of next ch-12 lp, work p, sl st in same ch-12 lp, ch 7,* sc in next sc) 6 times; rep bet *s once; sl st in first sc of rnd. Fasten off.

Feathery Snowflake

Approximately 3¾" in diameter

Materials:

DMC Cebelia #20, 7 yds.
Size 10 steel crochet hook

Ch 10; join with sl st in first ch to form ring.

Rnd 1: Ch 1, 24 sc in ring; sl st in first sc of rnd.

Rnd 2: Ch 4 (counts as dc and ch 1), (dc in next sc, ch 1) 23 times; sl st in 3rd ch of beg ch 4.

Rnd 3: Sl st in next ch-1 sp, *ch 4, 4 tr in same sp, ch 4, sl st in same sp, (ch 1, sc in next ch-1 sp) 3 times, sl st in next ch-1 sp; rep from *around, ending with sl st at base of beg ch 4.

Rnd 4: Work sl st and ch 1 up beg ch 4 to top, sl st in next tr, (sc bet 2 center tr of group, ch 7, sc in center sc bet tr-groups, ch 7) 6 times; sl st in first sc of rnd.

Rnd 5: *(*Ch 9, sl st in 9th ch from hook for picot*) 5 times, sl st in 3rd p, work p, sl st in 2nd p, work p, sl st in first p, sl st in sc at base of picots, ch 9, sc in next sc, work p, sc in same sp, ch 9,** sc in next sc; rep from * 4 times; rep from * to ** once; sl st in first sl st of rnd. Fasten off.

Dainty Snowflake

Approximately 2¼" in diameter

Materials:

DMC Cebelia #20, 4 yds.
Size 10 steel crochet hook

Ch 10; join with sl st in first ch to form ring.

Rnd 1: Ch 1, 18 sc in ring; sl st in first sc of rnd.

Rnd 2: Ch 10 (counts as dc and ch 7), (skip 2 dc, dc in next dc, ch 7) 5 times, skip 2 dc; sl st in 3rd ch of beg ch 10.

Rnd 3: Ch 1, in same sp *work sc, hdc, dc, tr, dtr, *ch 9, sl st in 9th ch from hook for picot,* tr, dc, hdc and sc,* ch 7, (rep bet *s once, ch 7) 5 times; sl st in first sc of rnd. Fasten off.

Picot Star

Approximately 3¼" in diameter

Materials:

DMC Cebelia #30, 11 yds.
Size 12 steel crochet hook

Ch 7; join with sl st in first ch to form ring.

Rnd 1: Ch 1, 15 sc in ring; sl st in first sc of rnd.

Rnd 2: Ch 5 (counts as dtr), dtr in same sp, 2 dtr in each of next 2 sc, ch 6, (2 dtr in each of next 3 sc, ch 6) 4 times; sl st in top of beg ch 5.

Rnd 3: Ch 1, sc in same sp, sc in each of next 5 dtr, (*in next ch-6 sp work sc, hdc, dc and tr, *ch 9, sl st in 9th ch from hook for picot,* work tr, dc, hdc and sc in same sp,* sc in each of next 6 dtr) 4 times; rep bet *s once; sl st in first sc of rnd.

Rnd 4: *Work sl st and ch 1 in each st to next p, (sc in p, work p) 2 times, sc in p, work 3 p, sl st in base of first of 3 p just worked, (sc in p, work p) 2 times, sc in p; rep from * 4 times; sl st in first sl st of rnd. Fasten off.

Picot Snowflake

Approximately 3" in diameter

Materials:

DMC Cebelia #30, 10 yds.
Size 12 steel crochet hook

Ch 9; join with sl st in first ch to form ring.

Rnd 1: Ch 3 (counts as dc), 23 dc in ring; sl st in top of beg ch 3.

Rnd 2: Ch 4 (counts as tr), tr in each of next 3 dc, ch 6, (tr in each of next 4 dc, ch 6) 5 times; sl st in top of beg ch 4.

Rnd 3: Ch 1, sc in same sp, and in each of next 3 tr, *in next ch-6 sp work sc, ch 1, hdc, ch 1, dc, ch 1, tr, ch 1, dc, ch 1, hdc, ch 1, sc,** sc in each of next 4 tr; rep from * 4 times; rep from * to ** once; sl st in first sc of rnd.

Rnd 4: *(Ch 1, sl st in next st) 3 times, (ch 1, sl st in next st, ch 1, sl st in next ch-1 sp) 3 times, sl st in tr, (*ch 9, sl st in 9th ch from hook for picot*) 5 times, sl st in base of first p made, (sl st in next ch-1 sp, ch 1, sl st in next st, ch 1) 3 times, sl st in next st; rep from * around. Fasten off.

Looped Snowflake

Approximately 3" in diameter

Materials:

DMC Cebelia, #20, 10 yds.
Size 10 steel crochet hook

Ch 9; join with sl st in first ch to form ring.

Rnd 1: Ch 3 (counts as dc), 2 dc in ring, (ch 4, 3 dc in ring) 5 times, ch 1, dc in top of beg ch-3 (this brings thread into position for next rnd).

Rnd 2: Ch 3 (counts as dc), 4 dc around post of dc just made, ch 4, (5 dc in next ch-4 sp, ch 4) 5 times; join in top of beg ch 3.

Rnd 3: Work ch 1 and sl st in each of next 4 dc, ch 1, (3 sc in next ch-3 sp, ch 9, 3 sc in same ch-3 sp, work sl st and ch 1 in each of next 5 dc) 5 times; 3 sc in next ch-4 sp, ch 9, 3 sc in same sp; sl st in first sl st.

Rnd 4: Work ch 1 and sl st in next 2 sl sts, ch 1, sc in same sp, *ch 6, sl st in 6th ch from hook for picot,* sc in same sp, ch 7, (*sc in next ch-9 lp, work p, sc in same lp, ch 7,* sc in center sl st of next group, work p, sc in same sp, ch 7) 5 times; rep bet *s once; sl st in first sc of rnd.

Rnd 5: Sl st to top of first p, ch 1, sc in same p, work p, sc in same sp, ch 9, (work sc, p and sc in next p, ch 9) 11 times; sl st in first sc of rnd. Fasten off.

Large Lacy Snowflake

Approximately 6½" in diameter

Materials:

DMC Cebelia #20, 28 yds.
Size 10 steel crochet hook

Ch 8; join with sl st in first ch to form ring.

Rnd 1: Ch 1, 12 sc in ring; sl st in first sc of rnd.

Rnd 2: Ch 1, sc in same sp and in next sc, (ch 12, sc in each of next 2 sc) 5 times, ch 5, yo 4 times and draw up a lp in first sc of rnd, (yo and draw through 2 lps) 5 times (this brings thread into position for next rnd).

Rnd 3: Ch 1, sc around post of st just made, (ch 12, sc in next ch-12 lp) 5 times; ch 12, tr in first sc of rnd.

Rnd 4: Ch 1, sc around post of st just made, (ch 9, sc in next ch-12 lp, ch 9, sc in same lp) 5 times, ch 9, sc in next ch-12 lp; ch 4, dtr in first sc of rnd.

Rnd 5: Ch 1, sc around post of st just made, (ch 12, sc in next ch-9 lp) 11 times; ch 5, yo 4 times and draw up a lp in first sc of rnd, (yo and draw through 2 lps) 5 times.

Rnd 6: Ch 1, sc around post of st just made, (ch 12, sc in next ch-12 lp) 11 times, ch 12; sl st in first sc of rnd.

Rnd 7: Ch 1, sc in same sp, (11 sc in next ch-12
(continued on the next page)

sp, sc in next sc) 11 times, 11 sc in next ch-12 sp; sl st in first sc of rnd.

Rnd 8: Ch 1, sc in same sp, (*ch 9, skip 5 sc, sc in next sc, ch 6, sc in same sc, ch 9, skip 5 sc, sc in next sc, ch 10, skip 5 sc, sc in next sc, ch 12, sc in same sc, ch 10, skip 5 sc,* sc in next sc) 5 times; rep bet *s once; sl st in first sc of rnd.

Rnd 9: Ch 1, sc in same sp, *(sc in ch-9 sp, ch 1) 4 times, sc in next sc, ch 1, sc in ch-6 sp, *ch 9,* *sl st in 9th ch from hook for picot,* ch 1, sc in same ch-6 lp, ch 1, sc in next sc, (ch 1, sc in ch-9 sp) 4 times, sc in next sc, (sc in ch-10 sp, ch 1) 6 times, sc in next sc, sc in ch-12 lp, ch 1, sc in same lp, work p, ch 1, sc in same ch-12 lp, work 5 p, sl st in 3rd p, work p, sl st in 2nd p, work p, sl st in first p, sc in ch-12 lp, ch 1, work p, sc in ch-12 lp, ch 1, sc in ch-12 lp, sc in next sc, (ch 1, sc in ch-10 sp) 6 times,** sc in next sc; rep from * 4 times; rep from * to ** once; sl st in first sc of rnd. Fasten off.

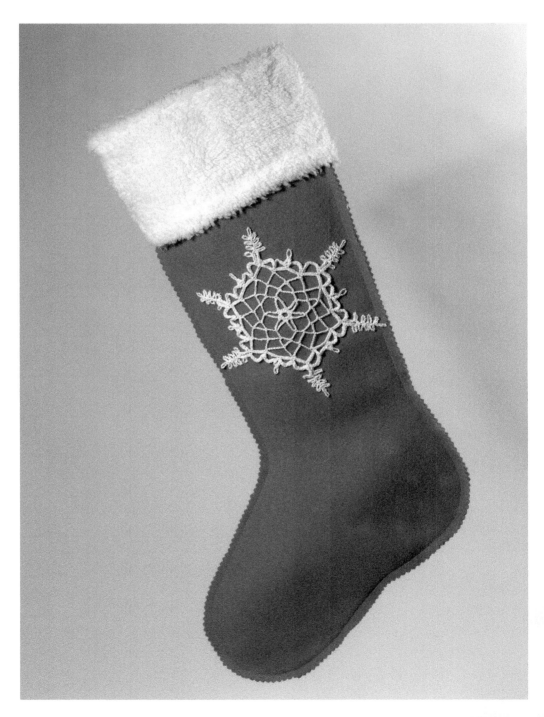

Shimmering Snowflake

Approximately 4¼" in diameter

Materials:

DMC Cebelia #30, 11 yds.
Size 12 steel crochet hook

Ch 12; join with sl st in first ch to form ring.

Rnd 1: Ch 1, 18 sc in ring; sl st in first sc of rnd.

Rnd 2: Ch 1, sc in same sp, (ch 12, skip 2 sc, sc in next sc) 5 times, ch 12, skip next 2 sc; sl st in first sc of rnd.

Rnd 3: Ch 1, sc in same sp, *(sl st in ch-12 lp, ch 1) 6 times, *ch 9, sl st in 9th ch from hook for picot*, (sl st in ch-12 lp, ch 1) 6 times,** sc in next sc; rep from * 4 times; rep from * to ** once; sl st in first sc of rnd. Fasten off.

Rnd 4: Join thread to top of any p, ch 1, sc in same sp, ch 20, (sc in top of next p, ch 20) 5 times; sl st in first sc of rnd.

Rnd 5: Ch 1, sc in same sp, *(sl st in ch-20 lp, ch 1) 10 times, work p, (sl st in ch-20 lp, ch 1) 10 times,** sc in next sc; rep from * 4 times; rep from * to ** once; sl st in first sc of rnd.

Rnd 6: Ch 1, sc in same sp, (*ch 15, sc in next p, ch 15, * sc in next sc) 5 times; rep bet *s once; sl st in first sc of rnd.

Rnd 7: Ch 1, sc in same sp, *(sl st in ch-15 lp, ch 1) 12 times, sl st in next p, work p, (sl st in ch-15 lp, ch 1) 12 times,** sc in next sc; rep from * 4 times; rep from * to ** once; sl st in first sc of rnd. Fasten off.

Teardrop

Approximately 3" by 3½"

Materials:

DMC Cebelia #20, 14 yds.
Size 10 steel crochet hook

Ch 10; join with sl st in first ch to form ring.

Rnd 1: Ch 1, 20 sc in ring; sl st in first sc of rnd.

Rnd 2: Ch 5 (counts as dtr), dtr in same sp, ch 1, (2 dtr in next sc, ch 1) 19 times; sl st in top of beg ch 5.

Rnd 3: *Do not work in ch-1 sps.* Ch 1, sc in same sp, ch 1, (sc in next st, ch 1) 3 times, (hdc in next st, ch 1) 4 times, (dc in next st, ch 1) 4 times, (tr in next st, ch 1) 4 times, (dtr in next st, ch 1) 8 times, (tr in next st, ch 1) 4 times, (dc in next st, ch 1) 4 times, (hdc in next st, ch 1) 4 times, (sc in next st, ch 1) 4 times; sl st in first sc of rnd.

Rnd 4: *Do not work in ch-1 sps.* Ch 2, dc in same sp, ch 4 (*yo, draw up a lp in next st, draw through 2 lps,* rep bet *s in next st, yo, draw through all 3 lps on hook, ch 4) 19 times; sl st in top of beg ch 2.

Rnd 5: Ch 1, *3 sc in next ch-4 sp, *ch 6, sl st in 6th ch from hook for picot, 3 sc in same ch-4 sp; rep from * around; sl st in first sc of rnd. Fasten off.

Layered Star

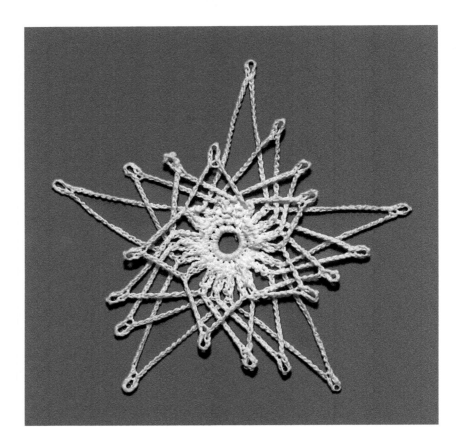

Approximately 3½" in diameter

Materials:

DMC Cebelia #30, 8 yds.
Size 12 steel crochet hook

Ch 10; join with sl st in first ch to form ring.

Rnd 1: Ch 1, 20 sc in ring; sl st in first sc of rnd.

Rnd 2: Ch 1, sc in same sp, *ch 6, sl st in 6th ch from hook for picot,* (sc in next sc, work p) 19 times; sl st in first sc of rnd.

Rnd 3: Sl st to top of first p, ch 1, sc in same p, (*ch 6, work p, ch 6, skip next 3 p*, sc in next p) 4 times; rep bet *s once; sl st in first sc of rnd.

Rnd 4: Holding loops of prev rnd to front, sl st to top of next p, ch 1, sc in same sp, (*ch 9, work p, ch 9, skip next 3 p*, sc in next p) 4 times; rep bet *s once; sl st in first sc of rnd.

Rnd 5: Holding all loops to front, sl st to top of next p, ch 1, sc in same p, (*ch 12, work p, ch 12, skip next 3 p,* sc in next p) 4 times; rep bet *s; sl st in first sc of rnd.

Rnd 6: Holding all loops to front, sl st to top of next p, ch 1, sc in same sp, (*ch 18, work p, ch 18, skip next 3 p,* sc in next p) 4 times; rep bet *s once; sl st in first sc of rnd. Fasten off.

Flower Snowflake

Approximately 4" in diameter

Materials:

DMC Cebelia #30, 11 yds.
Size 12 steel crochet hook

Ch 12; join with sl st in first ch to form ring.

Rnd 1: Ch 2 (counts as first hdc), 17 hdc in ring; sl st in top of first ch 2—18 hdc.

Rnd 2: Ch 1, sc in same sp, ch 20, skip next 2 hdc, (sc in next hdc, ch 20, skip next 2 hdc) 5 times; sl st in first sc of rnd.

Rnd 3: Ch 1, sc in same sp, (*in ch-20 lp work 3 sc, 3 hdc, 3 dc, 5 tr, 3 dc, 3 hdc and 3 sc,* sc in next hdc) 5 times; rep bet *s once; sl st in first sc of rnd.

Rnd 4: Sl st in next 5 sts, ch 1, *sc in each of next 6 sts to center tr, sc in center tr, ch 9, sc in same sp, sc in each of next 6 sts, skip next 5 sts of same lp,** skip sc bet lps and next 5 sts of next lp; rep from * 5 times; rep from * to ** once; sl st in first sc of rnd.

Rnd 5: Ch 1, work sl st and ch 1 in each sc to ch-9 lp, *(2 sc in ch-9 lp, *ch 9, sl st in 9th ch from hook for picot*) 3 times, 2 sc in same lp,** work sl st and ch 1 in each sc to next ch-9 lp, rep from * 5 times, rep from * to ** once; work sl st and ch 1 in each sc to beg of rnd. Fasten off.

Small Heart

Approximately 2¼" x 2¼"

Materials:

DMC Cebelia #20, 7 yds.
Size 10 steel crochet hook

Ch 9; join with sl st in first ch to form ring.

Rnd 1: Ch 4 (counts as hdc and ch 2), in ring, work tr, ch 3, (dtr, ch 3) twice, tr, ch 3, (dc, ch 3) twice, tr, ch 3, dtr, ch 3, tr, ch 3, (dc, ch 3) twice, tr, ch 3, (dtr, ch 3) twice, tr, ch 2; sl st in 2nd ch of beg ch 4.

Rnd 2: Ch 1, sc, *2 sc in next ch-sp, *ch 6, sl st in* 6th ch from hook for picot, 2 sc in same ch-sp; rep from * around; sl st in first sc of rnd.

Rnd 3: Work sl st and ch 1 to top of first p, ch 1, sc in same p, work p, sc in same p, ch 2, work sc, p, sc and ch 2 in each p around; sl st in first sc of rnd. Fasten off.

12-Pointed Ornament

Approximately 3¼" in diameter

Materials:

DMC Cebelia #30, 11 yds.
Size 12 steel crochet hook

Ch 9; join with sl st in first ch to form ring.

Rnd 1: Ch 1, 12 sc in ring; sl st in first sc of rnd.

Rnd 2: Ch 1, sc in same sc, ch 20, (sc in next sc, ch 20) 11 times; sl st in first sc of rnd. Fasten off.

Rnd 3: Join thread in top of any lp, ch 1, sc in same lp, (*sc in next lp, ch 6, *ch 6, sl st in 6th ch from hook for picot,* ch 6,* sc in same lp) 11 times; rep bet *s once; sl st in first sc of rnd.

Rnd 4: Ch 1, sc in same sp, sc in next sc, (*7 sc in next ch-6 sp, work sl st and ch 1 to top of p, sc in p, work p, sc in same p, work sl st and ch 1 down p, 7 sc in same ch-6 sp,* sc in each of next 2 sc) 11 times; rep bet *s once; sl st in first sc of rnd. Fasten off.

Jeweled Snowflake

Approximately 2¾" in diameter

Materials:

DMC Cebelia #20, 10 yds.
Size 10 steel crochet hook

Ch 12; join with sl st in first ch to form ring.

Rnd 1: Ch 1, 24 sc in ring; sl st in first sc of rnd.

Rnd 2: Ch 3 (counts as dc), dc in each of next 3 sc, ch 7, (dc in each of next 4 sc, ch 7) 5 times; sl st in top of beg ch 3.

Rnd 3: Ch 1, sc in same sp, (*ch 3, skip 2 sc, sc in next sc, 4 sc in next ch-7 sp, *ch 9, sl st in 9th ch from hook for picot*, 4 sc in ch-7 sp,* sc in

next sc) 5 times; rep, bet *s once; sl st in first sc of rnd.

Rnd 4: Ch 1, sc in same sp, *sc in next ch-3 sp, work p, sc in same ch-3 sp, sc in next sc, ch 7, skip 4 sc, sl st in base of next p, 2 sc in p, (work p, sc in same p of prev rnd) 3 times, sl st in base of p of prev rnd, ch 7, skip 4 sc,** sc in next sc; rep from * 4 times; rep from * to ** once; sl st in first sc of rnd. Fasten off.

Blossom Snowflake

Approximately 3½" in diameter

Materials:

DMC Cebelia #20, 12 yds.
Size 10 steel crochet hook

Ch 9; join with sl st in first ch to form ring.

Rnd 1: Ch 2 (counts as hdc), 11 hdc in ring; sl st in top of beg ch 2.

Rnd 2: Ch 8 (counts as dc and ch 5), (skip 1 hdc, dc in next dc, ch 5) 5 times; sl st in 3rd ch of beg ch 8.

Rnd 3: Ch 3 (counts as dc), (6 dc in next ch-5 sp, dc in next dc) 5 times, 6 dc in next ch-5 sp; sl st in top of beg ch 3.

Rnd 4: Ch 24 (counts as tr and ch 20), (skip 6 dc, tr in next dc, ch 20) 5 times, skip 6 dc; sl st in 4th ch of beg ch 24.

Rnd 5: Ch 6 (counts as dc and ch 3), *(dc in next ch-20 lp, ch 3) 6 times,** dc in next tr, ch 3; rep from * 4 times; rep from * to ** once; sl st in 3rd ch of beg ch 6.

Rnd 6: Ch 1, 3 sc in each ch-3 sp around; sl st in first sc of rnd. Fasten off.

Pineapple Star Suncatcher

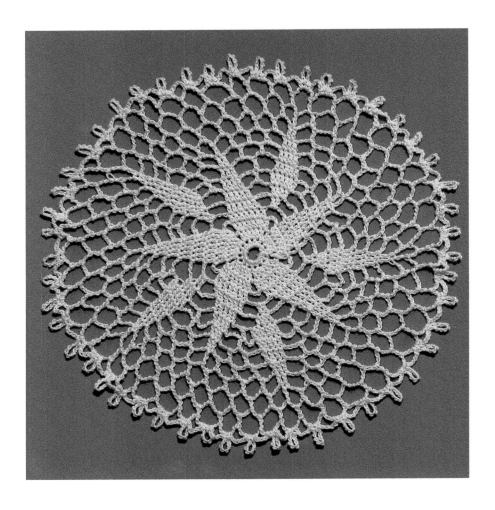

Approximately 7" in diameter

Materials:

DMC Cebelia #20, 50 yds.
Size 10 steel crochet hook

Ch 10; join with sl st in first ch to form ring.

Rnd 1: Ch 2 (counts as hdc), 14 hdc in ring; sl st in top of beg ch 2.

Rnd 2: Ch 3 (counts as dc), dc in same sp, 2 dc in each of next 2 hdc, (ch 2, 2 dc in each of next 3 hdc) 4 times, ch 2; sl st in top of beg ch 3.

Rnd 3: Ch 3 (counts as dc), dc in same sp, dc in each of next 4 dc, 2 dc in next dc, ch 3, skip ch-2 sp, (2 dc in next dc, dc in each of next 4 dc, 2 dc in next ch, ch 3) 4 times; sl st in top of beg ch 3.

Rnd 4: Sl st in next dc (counts as dc), ch 3, dc in each of next 6 dc, ch 5, (skip ch-3 sp and next dc, dc in each of next 7 dc, ch 5) 4 times; sl st in top of beg ch 3.

Rnd 5: Sl st in next dc, ch 3 (counts as dc), dc in each of next 5 dc, ch 5, 2 dc in next ch-5 sp, ch 5, (skip next dc, dc in each of next 6 dc, ch 5, 2 dc in next ch-5 sp, ch 5) 4 times; sl st in top of beg ch 3.

Rnd 6: Sl st in next dc, ch 3 (counts as dc), dc in each of next 4 dc, *ch 6, skip ch-5 sp, 2 dc in each of next 2 dc, ch 6,* (skip ch-5 sp and next dc, dc in each of next 5 dc, rep bet *s) 4 times; sl st in top of beg ch 3.

Rnd 7: Sl st in next dc, ch 3 (counts as dc), dc in each of next 3 dc, ch 3, dc in next ch-6 sp, ch 3, (2 dc in next dc, dc in each of next 2 dc, 2 dc in next dc, ch 3, dc in next ch-6 sp, ch 3, skip next dc, dc in each of next 4 dc; ch 3, dc in next ch-6 sp, ch 3) 4 times, 2 dc in next dc, dc in each of next 2 dc, 2 dc in next dc, ch 3, dc in next ch-6 sp, ch 3; sl st in top of beg ch 3.

(continued on the next page)

Rnd 8: Sl st in next dc, ch 3 (counts as dc), dc in each of next 2 dc, ch 5, dc in next dc, ch 5, (*skip next dc, dc in each of next 5 dc, ch 5, dc in next dc, ch 5,* skip next dc, dc in each of next 3 dc, ch 5, dc in next dc, ch 5) 4 times, rep from * to * once; sl st in top of beg ch 3.

Rnd 9: Sl st in next dc, ch 3 (counts as dc), dc in next dc, *(ch 4, dc in next ch-5 sp) 2 times, ch 4, skip next dc, dc in each of next 4 dc, ch 4, (dc in next ch-5 sp, ch 4) 2 times,** skip next dc, dc in each of next 2 dc; rep from * 3 times, rep * to ** once; sl st in top of beg ch 3.

Rnd 10: Ch 7 (counts as dc and ch 4), (dc in next ch-4 sp, ch 4) 3 times, *skip next dc, dc in each of next 3 dc, (ch 4, dc in next ch-4 sp) 3 times, ch 4,** skip next dc, dc in next dc, (ch 4, dc in ch-4 sp) 3 times, ch 4; rep from * 3 times, rep * to **; sl st in 3rd ch of beg ch 7.

Rnd 11: Sl st in next 2 chs, ch 8 (counts as dc and ch 5), (dc in next ch-4 sp, ch 5) 3 times, *skip next dc, dc in each of next 2 dc, (ch 5, dc in next ch-4 sp) 8 times, ch 5; rep from * 3 times, skip next dc, dc in each of next 2 dc, (ch 5, dc in ch-4 sp) 4 times, ch 5; sl st in 3rd ch of beg ch 8.

Rnd 12: Sl st in next 3 chs, ch 9 (counts as dc and ch 6), (dc in next ch-sp, ch 6) 2 times, dc in next ch-sp, *ch 4, skip next dc, dc in next dc, ch 4, dc in next ch-5 sp, (ch 6, dc in next ch-5 sp) 8 times; rep from * 3 times, ch 4, skip next dc, dc in next dc, ch 4, (dc in next ch-5 sp, ch 6) 5 times; sl st in 3rd ch of beg ch 9.

Rnd 13: Sl st in next 3 chs, ch 10 (counts as dc and ch 7), (dc in next ch-sp, ch 7) around; sl st in 3rd ch of beg ch 10.

Rnd 14: Sl st in next 3 chs, ch 1, sc in same ch-sp, *ch 9, sl st in 9th ch from hook for picot,* sc in same ch-sp as last sc, ch 5, *sc in next ch-7 sp, work picot, sc in same ch-7 sp, ch 5; rep from * around; sl st in first sc of rnd. Fasten off.

Leaf Garland

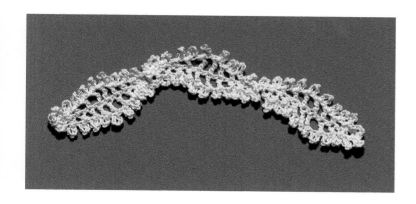

Each leaf, 1" by 1½"

Materials:

DMC Cebelia #30, 3 yds. per leaf.
Size 12 steel crochet hook

†Ch 21.
Sc in 2nd ch from hook, *ch 6, sl st in 6th ch from hook for picot,* *skip next ch, work sc and p in next ch, skip next ch, work hdc and p in next ch, skip next ch, work dc and p in next ch, (skip next ch, work tr and p in next ch) twice, skip next ch, work dc and p in next ch, skip next ch, work hdc and p in next ch, (skip next ch, work sc and p in next ch) twice, sc in next sc,* 3 sc in next ch for point; working on opposite side of starting ch, sc in next ch, work p; rep bet *s— leaf completed; *do not fasten off*. Repeat from † for desired length. Fasten off.

Mesh Snowflake

Approximately 3" in diameter

Materials:

DMC Cebelia #30, 9 yds.
Size 12 steel crochet hook

Ch 10; join with sl st in first ch to form ring.

Rnd 1: Ch 1, 12 sc in ring; sl st in first sc of rnd.

Rnd 2: Ch 6 (counts as dc and ch 3), (dc in next sc, ch 3) 11 times; sl st in 3rd ch of beg ch 6.

Rnd 3: Ch 9 (counts as tr and ch 5), (tr in next dc, ch 5) 11 times; sl st in 4th ch of beg ch 11.

Rnd 4: Ch 7 (counts as tr and ch 3), (tr in next ch-5 sp, ch 3, tr in next tr, ch 3) 11 times, tr in next ch-5 sp, ch 3; sl st in 4th ch of beg ch 7.

Rnd 5: Ch 1, *work 3 sc and hdc in next ch-3 sp, work dc and 2 tr in next ch-3 sp, (*ch 6, sl st in 6th ch from hook for picot*) 3 times, sl st in last tr made, work 2 tr and dc in next ch-3 sp, work hdc and 3 sc in next ch-3 sp; rep from * 5 times; sl st in first sc of rnd. Fasten off.

Crown Snowflake

Approximately 2¾" in diameter

Materials:

DMC Cebelia #30, 7 yds.
Size 12 steel crochet hook

Ch 9; join with sl st in first ch to form ring.

Rnd 1: Ch 1, 12 sc in ring; sl st in first sc of rnd.

Rnd 2: Ch 7 (counts as dtr and ch 2), dtr in next sc, (ch 6, dtr in next sc, ch 2, dtr in next sc) 5 times, ch 6; sl st in 5th ch of beg ch 7.

Rnd 3: Ch 1, (in next ch-2 sp work sc, hdc, dc, hdc, sc; sc in next ch-6 sp, ch 6, 2 dtr in same sp, ch 6, sc in same sp) 6 times; sl st in first sc of rnd.

Rnd 4: Ch 1, sc in same sc, (sc in each of next 2 sts, *ch 9, sl st in 9th ch from hook for picot*, sc in each of next 2 sts, skip next sc, ch 9, sc bet next 2 dtr, work p, sc in same sp, ch 9,* skip next sc, sc in next sc) 5 times; rep bet *s once; sl st in first sc of rnd. Fasten off.

Regal Snowflake

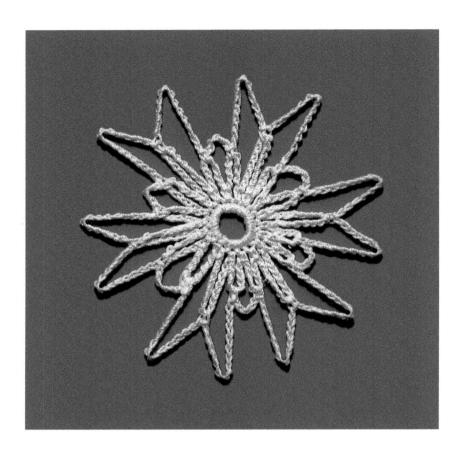

Approximately 2¼" in diameter

Materials:

DMC Cebelia #20, 5 yds.
Size 10 steel crochet hook

Ch 9; join with sl st in first ch to form ring.

Rnd 1: Ch 1, 18 sc in ring; sl st in first sc of rnd.

Rnd 2: Ch 1, sc in same sp, *ch 15, (sc in next sc, ch 9) 2 times, sc in next sc; rep from * 4 times; ch 15, sc in next sc, ch 9, sc in next sc, ch 4, dtr in first sc of rnd (this brings thread into position for next rnd).

Rnd 3: Ch 1, sc around post of dtr just made, (*ch 15, sc in next ch-15 lp, ch 15, sc in next ch-9 lp, ch 5,* sc in next ch-9 lp) 5 times; rep bet *s once; sl st, in first sc of rnd. Fasten off.

Scalloped Wreath

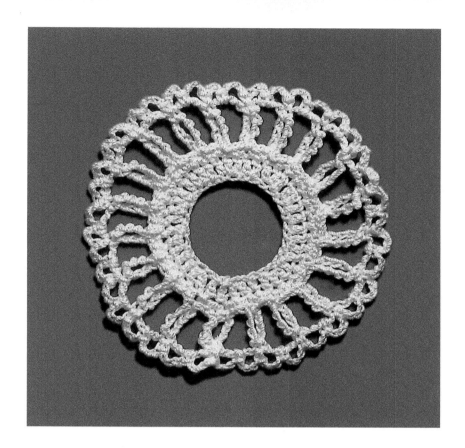

Approximately 2¾" in diameter

Materials:

DMC Cebelia #20, 10 yds.
Size 10 steel crochet hook

Ch 32; join with sl st in first ch to form ring, being careful not to twist ch.

Rnd 1: Ch 3 (Counts as dc), dc in next ch, (2 dc in next ch, dc in each of next 2 ch) 10 times; sl st in top of beg ch 3—32 dc.

Rnd 2: Ch 1, 2 sc in same sp, sc in next dc, *ch 9, sl st in 9th ch from hook for picot,* *2 sc in next dc, sc in next dc, work p; rep from * around; sl st in first sc of rnd.

Rnd 3: Work sl st and ch 1 up first p to top, ch 1, sc in same sp, ch 4, *sc in next p, ch 4; rep from * around; sl st in first sc of rnd.

Rnd 4: Ch 1, sc in same sp, (ch 3, sc in next ch-4 sp, ch 3, sc in next sc) 20 times, ch 3, sc in next ch-4 sp, ch 3; sl st in first sc. Fasten off.

Spiderweb Suncatcher

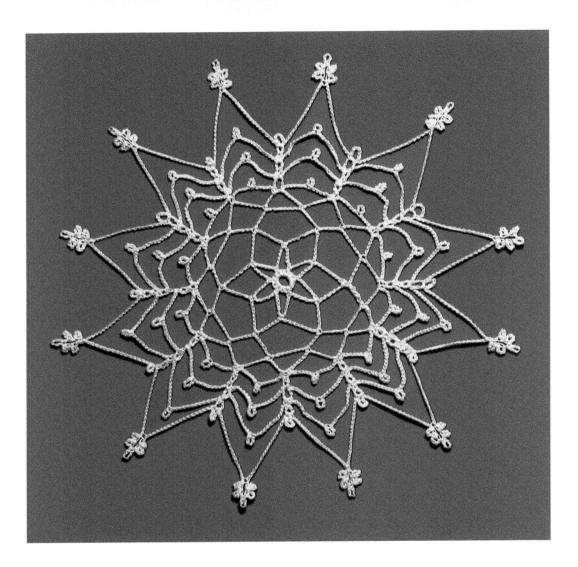

Approximately 8" in diameter

Materials:

DMC Cebelia #20, 29 yds.
Size 10 steel crochet hook

Ch 9; join with sl st in first ch to form ring.

Rnd 1: Ch 1, 12 sc in ring, sl st in top of first sc.

Rnd 2: Ch 1, sc in same sp, (ch 12, skip next sc, sc in next sc) 5 times; ch 6, yo hook 4 times and draw up a lp in first sc of rnd, (yo and draw through 2 lps) 5 times (this brings thread into postion for next rnd).

Rnd 3: Ch 1, sc around post of st just made, (ch 15, sc in next ch-12 lp) 5 times; ch 7, yo hook 5 times and draw up a lp in first sc of rnd, (yo and draw through 2 lps) 6 times.

Rnd 4: Ch 1, sc around post of st just made, ch 18, (sc in next ch-15 lp, ch 18) 5 times; sl st in first sc of rnd.

(continued on the next page)

Rnd 5: Sl st in each of next 5 chs, ch 1, sc in same ch-18 lp, ch 12, sc in same lp, ch 12, (sc in next ch-18 lp, ch 12, sc in same lp, ch 12) 5 times; sl st in first sc of rnd.

Rnd 6: Sl st in each of next 5 chs, ch 1, sc in same ch-12 lp, *ch 6, sl st in 6th ch from hook for picot,* sc in same ch-12 lp, ch 6, work p, ch 6, (sc in next ch-12 lp, work p, sc in same ch-12 lp, ch 6, work p, ch 6) 11 times; sl st in first sc of rnd.

Rnd 7: Work sl st and ch 1 to top of first p, ch 1, sc in same p, work p, sc in same p, ch 9, work p, ch 9, skip next p, (sc in next p, work p, sc in same p, ch 9, work p, ch 9, skip next p) 11 times; sl st in first sc of rnd.

Rnd 8: Work sl st and ch 1 to top of first p, ch 1, sc in same p, work p, sc in same p, (*ch 12, work p, ch 12, skip next p,* sc in next p, work p, sc in same p) 11 times; rep bet *s once; sl st in first sc of rnd.

Rnd 9: Work sl st and ch 1 to top of first p, ch 1, sc in same p, work p, sc in same p, (*ch 18, work 5 p, sl st in ch just below base of first p, ch 17, skip next p,* sc in next p, work p, sc in same p) 11 times; rep bet *s once; sl st in first sc of rnd. Fasten off.

Trefoil Snowflake

Approximately 3½" in diameter

Materials:

DMC Cebelia #30, 7 yds.
Size 12 steel crochet hook

Ch 10; join with sl st in first ch to form ring.

Rnd 1: Ch 1, 18 sc in ring; sl st in first sc of rnd.

Rnd 2: Ch 1, sc in same sp, ch 18, skip next 2 sc, (sc in next sc, ch 18, skip next 2 sc) 5 times; sl st in first sc of rnd.

Rnd 3: Ch 1, *10 sc in next ch-18 lp, ch 6, *(ch 9, sl st in 9th ch from hook for picot)* 3 times, ch 6, 10 sc in same ch-18 lp; rep from * 5 times; sl st in first sc of rnd. Fasten off.

Sunflower Ornament

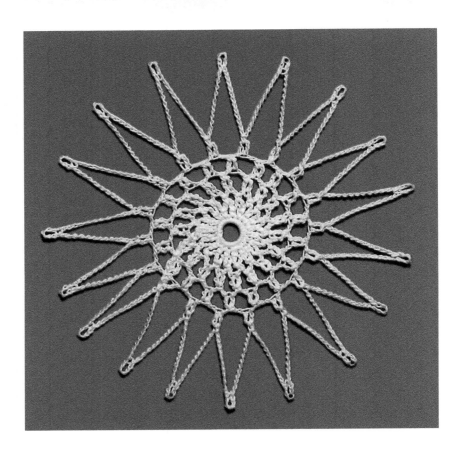

Approximately 4½" in diameter

Materials:

DMC Cebelia #30, 13 yds.
Size 12 steel crochet hook

Ch 12; join with sl st in first ch to form ring.

Rnd 1: Ch 1, work 18 sc in ring; sl st in first sc of rnd.

Rnd 2: Ch 1, sc in same sp, ch 6, (sc in next sc, ch 6) 16 times, sc in next sc, ch 3, dc in first sc of rnd (this brings thread into position for next rnd).

Rnd 3: Ch 1, sc around post of dc just made, ch 1, *ch 6, sl st in 6th ch from hook for picot,* ch 1, (sc in next ch-6 sp, ch 1, work p, ch 1) 17 times; sl st in first sc of rnd.

Rnd 4: Work sl st and ch 1 to top of first p, ch 1, sc in same p, ch 1, work p, ch 1, (sc in next p, ch 1, work p, ch 1) 17 times; sl st in first sc of rnd.

Rnd 5: Repeat rnd 4.

Rnd 6: Work sl st and ch 1 to top of first p, ch 1, sc in same p, ch 12, work p, ch 12, (sc in next p, ch 12, work p, ch 12) 17 times; sl st in first sc of rnd. Fasten off.

Round Star

Approximately 3¾" in diameter

Materials:

DMC Cebelia #10, 21 yds.
Size 7 steel crochet hook

Ch 10; join with a sl st in first ch to form ring.

Rnd 1: Ch 3 (counts as dc), 19 dc in ring; join in top of beg ch 3.

Rnd 2: Ch 1, sc and hdc in same sp, (*work dc, tr, and dtr in next dc, work dtr, tr and dc in next dc, work hdc and sc in next dc,* work sc and hdc in next dc) 4 times; rep bet *s once; join in first sc—50 sts.

Rnd 3: *Ch 5, skip next st, sl st in next st; rep from * around, ending with ch 2, dc in joining of last rnd (this brings thread into position for next rnd).

Rnd 4: Ch 1, sc around dc just made, *ch 5, sl st in next ch-5 sp; rep from * around, ending with ch 2, dc in first sc.

Rnd 5: Rep rnd 4, ending with ch 5, sl st in first sc

Rnd 6: Ch 1, work 3 sc and ch 1 in each ch-5 sp around; join.

Rnd 7: Ch 2 (counts as hdc), hdc in each of next 2 sc, *hdc in next ch-1 sp, hdc in each of next 3 hdc; rep from * around, ending with hdc in last ch-1 sp; join.

Rnd 8: Work sl st and ch 1 in each hdc around; join and fasten off.

Ruffled Wreath

Approximately 3¼" in diameter

Materials:

DMC Cebelia #10, 40 yds.
Size 7 steel crochet hook
½ yd. ³⁄₁₆"-wide ribbon

Ch 45; join with sl st in first ch to form ring, being very careful not to twist chain.

Rnd 1: Ch 1, sc in same sp and in each ch around; join in first sc.

Rnd 2: Ch 5 (counts as dc and ch 2); working in front lps only of sts, dc in same sp, ch 2, work dc, ch 2, dc and ch 2 in each sc around; join in 3rd ch of beg ch 5.

Rnd 3: Sl st down back of work to base of beg ch. With right side facing, working in back lps only of sts, (sc in next sc, 2 sc in next sc) 22 times, sc in last sc; join.

Rnd 4: Ch 5, turn; working in front lps only of sts, dc in same sp, ch 2, work dc, ch 2, dc and ch 2 in each sc around; join in 3rd ch of beg ch 5.

Rnd 5: Turn, sl st down back of work to base of beg ch, ch 6, working in back lps only of sts, tr in same sp, ch 2, work tr, ch 2, tr and ch 2 in each st around; join in 4th ch of beg ch 6 and fasten off.

Starch the wreath. Tie a ribbon bow; tack it to the wreath.

Spiderweb Snowflake

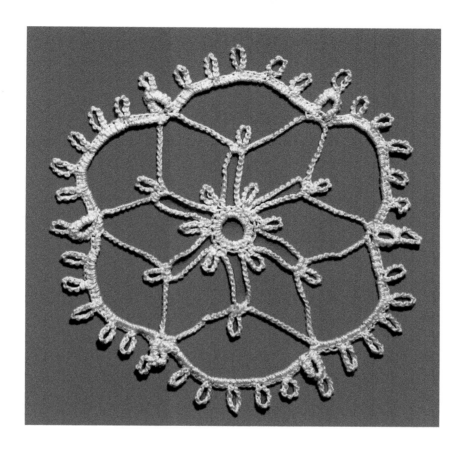

Approximately 4½" in diameter

Materials:

DMC Cebelia #20, 16 yds.
Size 10 steel crochet hook

Ch 12; join with sl st in first ch to form ring.

Rnd 1: Ch 2 (counts as hdc), 17 hdc in ring; sl st in top of beg ch 2.

Rnd 2: Ch 1, (sc in next hdc, *ch 9, sl st in 9th ch from hook for picot,* sc in next hdc, ch 20, skip 1 hdc) 6 times; sl st in first sc of rnd. Fasten off.

Rnd 3: Join thread to top of any ch-20 lp, ch 1, sc in same lp, (*work p, sc in same lp, ch 25,* sc in next ch-20 lp) 5 times, rep bet *s once; sl st in first sc of rnd. Fasten off.

Rnd 4: Join thread to top of any ch-20 lp, ch 1, sc in same lp, (*work p, sc in same lp, ch 20,* sc in next ch-20 lp) 5 times, rep bet *s once; sl st in first sc of rnd.

Rnd 5: Ch 1, sc in same sp, *work sl st and ch 1 up p to top, ch 1, work sc, p and sc in top of p, work sl st and ch 1 down other side of p, sc in next sc, in next ch-25 lp work (4 sc, p) 5 times, 4 sc in same lp,** sc in next sc; rep from * 4 times; rep from * to ** once; sl st in first sc of rnd. Fasten off.

Openwork Star

Approximately 6½" in diameter

Materials:

DMC Cebelia #20, 11 yds.
Size 10 steel crochet hook

Ch 10; join with sl st in first ch to form ring.

Rnd 1: Ch 1 (counts as hdc), 13 hdc in ring; sl st in top of beg ch 2—14 hdc.

Rnd 2: Ch 1, sc in same sp, (*ch 15, sl st in 2nd and 3rd ch from hook for point, ch 13, skip next hdc, * sc in next hdc) 6 times; rep bet *s once; sl st in first sc of rnd.

Rnd 3: Work sl st and ch 1 up ch 15 to point, ch 1, sc in same point, (*ch 20, sl st in 2nd, 3rd, and 4th ch from hook for point, ch 17,* sc in next point) 6 times; rep bet *s once; sl st in first sc of rnd.

Rnd 4: Work sl st and ch 1 up ch 17 to point, ch 1, sc in same point, (*ch 25, sl st in 2nd, 3rd, and 4th ch from hook for point, ch 22,* sc in next point) 6 times; rep bet *s once; sl st in first sc of rnd. Fasten off.

Ruffled Circle

Approximately 2¾" in diameter

Materials:

DMC Cebelia #10, 22 yds.
Size 7 steel crochet hook

Ch 6; join with sl st in first ch to form ring.

Rnd 1: Ch 4 (counts as dc and ch 1), (work dc and ch 1) 11 times in ring, join with sl st in 3rd ch of beg ch 4—12 dc.

Rnd 2: Ch 1, 2 sc in same sp, sc in ch-1 sp, (2 sc in next sc, sc in next ch-1) 11 times; join in first sc—36 sc.

Rnd 3: Working in front lps only of sts, ch 5 (counts as dc and ch 2), dc in same sp, ch 2, work dc, ch 2, dc and ch 2 in each st around; join in 3rd ch of ch 5.

Rnd 4: Sl st down back of work to rnd 2, ch 6, work tr and ch 2 in each st around; join in 4th ch of beg ch 6.

Rnd 5: Ch 1, *sc in next ch-2 sp, 2 sc in next ch-2 sp; rep from * around; join in first sc—54 sc.

Rnd 6: Ch 5, dc in same sp, ch 2, work dc and ch 2 in each sc around; join in 3rd ch of beg ch 5; fasten off.

Ruffled Star

Approximately 4" in diameter

Materials:

DMC Cebelia #10, 34 yds.
Size 7 steel crochet hook

Ch 5; join with sl st in first ch to form ring.

Rnd 1: Ch 1, 10 sc in ring; join with sl st in first sc.

Rnd 2: Ch 3 (counts as dc), dc in same sp, 2 dc in each sc around; join in top of beg ch 3—20 dc.

Rnd 3: Ch 3; working in back lps only of sts, dc in same sp, 2 dc in each dc around; join in beg ch 3—40 dc.

Rnd 4: Ch 1; working in both lps of sts, sc in same sp, (*hdc in next dc, dc in next dc, work tr and 2 dtr in next dc, work 2 dtr and tr in next dc, dc in next dc, hdc in next dc*, sc in each of next 2 dc) 4 times; rep bet *s once, sc in next sc; join in first sc—60 sts.

Rnd 5: Ch 4 (counts as dc and ch 1), work dc and ch 1 in next st and in each st around; join in 3rd ch of beg ch 4.

Rnd 6: Sl st in next ch-1 sp, ch 4, work dc in same sp, ch 1, work dc, ch 1, dc and ch 1 in each ch-1 sp around; join in 3rd ch of beg ch 4.

Rnd 7: Sl st in next ch-1 sp, ch 1, sc in same sp, ch 4, work sc and ch 4 in each ch-1 sp around; join in first sc.

(continued on the next page)

Rnd 8: Sl st in first ch of ch-4, ch 1, sc in same sp, ch 5, work sc and ch 5 in each ch-4 sp around; join and fasten off.

Center: Inserting hook through st from center of piece to outer edge, join thread to front lp of any st of rnd 2.

Rnd 1: Ch 3, dc in same sp, ch 1, work 2 dc and ch 1 in each st around; join in top of beg ch 3.

Rnd 2: Sl st in next dc and ch-1 sp, ch 1, sc in same sp, ch 4; work sc and ch 4 in each ch-1 sp around; join and fasten off.

Icicle Snowflake

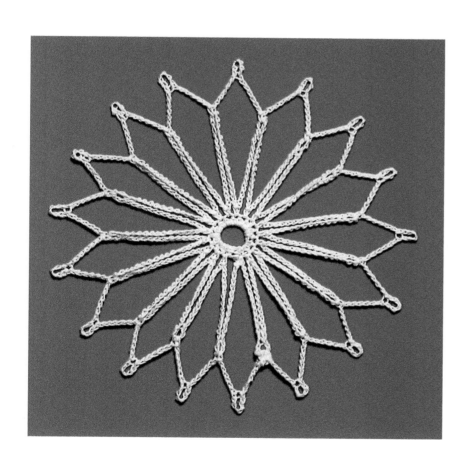

Approximately 4¼" in diameter

Materials:

DMC Cebelia #20, 11 yds.
Size 10 steel crochet hook

Ch 10; join with sl st in first ch to form ring.

Rnd 1: Ch 2 (counts as hdc), 16 hdc in ring; sl st in top of beg ch 2.

Rnd 2: Ch 1, sc in same sp, (*ch 12, *ch 6, sl st in 6th ch from hook for picot, ch 12,* sc in next hdc) 16 times, rep bet *s once; sl st in first sc of rnd. Fasten off.

Rnd 3: Join thread to top of any p, ch 1, sc in same sp (ch 6, work p, ch 6; sc in next p) 17 times; rep bet *s once; sl st in first sc of rnd. Fasten off.

Fancy Star

Approximately 2" in diameter

Materials:

DMC Cebelia # 10, 9 yds.
Size 7 steel crochet hook

Ch 7, join with sl st in first ch to form ring.

Rnd 1: Ch 1, work 15 sc in ring; join in first sc.

Rnd 2: Ch 1, sc and hdc in same sp, (*work dc, tr and dc in next sc, hdc and sc in next sc*, sc and hdc in next sc) 4 times, rep bet *s once; join in first sc—35 sts.

Rnd 3: Ch 1, sc in same sp, (*hdc in next st, 2 dc in next st, 4 tr in next tr, 2 dc in next st, hdc in next st*, sc in each of next 2 sts) 4 times; rep bet *s once, sc in last sc; join in first sc—60 sts.

Rnd 4: Sl st in next st, ch 1, sc in same sp, ch 1, work sc and ch 1 in each of next 9 sts, skip next 2 sc; *sc and ch 1 in each of next 10 sps, skip next 2 sc; rep from *around; join in first sc and fasten off.

Tiny Bells

Approximately 1½" in diameter, 1" high

Materials:

DMC Cebelia #10, 26 yds. Three large beads
Size 7 steel crochet hook Sewing thread
1 yd. ⅛"-wide ribbon

Make 3 bells.

Ch 5; join with sl st in first ch to form ring.

Rnd 1: Ch 1, 10 sc in ring; join in first sc.

Rnd 2: Ch 1, 2 sc in same sc, 2 sc in each rem sc; join in first sc—20 sc.

Rnds 3–8: Ch 2 (counts as hdc), hdc in next st and in each st around.

Rnd 9: Ch 1, sc in same st, (hdc and dc in next hdc, dc and hdc in next hdc, sc in each of next 2 hdc) 4 times, hdc and dc in next hdc, dc and hdc

in next hdc, sc in last hdc; join in first sc.

Rnd 10: Ch 1, sc in same st, ch 1, *sc in next st, ch 1; rep from * around; join and fasten off.

Starch the bells. Attach each of the three beads to a length of thread. From the inside, insert the thread through the top of the bell; adjust so that the bead hangs freely. Attach securely, cutting off the extra thread. Repeat with all bells. Sew a small ribbon bow to top of each bell.

Scalloped Wreath

Approximately 2¼" in diameter

Materials:

DMC Cebelia #10, 22 yds.
Size 7 steel crochet hook

Ch 24; join with sl st in first ch to form ring, being careful not to twist ch.

Rnd 1: Ch 1, sc in same sp, 2 sc in next sc, (sc in next sc, 2 sc in next sc) 11 times; join in first sc—36 sc.

Rnd 2: Working in front lps only of sts, ch 1, sc in same sp, *work hdc, dc and tr in next sc, work tr, dc and hdc in next sc, sc in each of next 2 sc; rep from * around, ending last rep with sc in last sc.

Rnd 3: Sl st down back of work to rnd 1, (sc in each of next 2 sc, 2 sc in next sc) 12 times; join in first sc—48 sc.

Rnd 4: Working in front lps only of sts, rep rnd 2.

Rnd 5: Sl st down back of work to rnd 3, ch 1, (sc in each of next 5 sc, 2 sc in next sc) 8 times; join in first sc—54 sc.

Rnd 6: Working in front lps of rnd 5; rep rnd 2; join and fasten off.

Inner Rnd: Join thread in any ch of beginning ch 24, ch 1, sc in same ch and in each ch around; join in first sc and fasten off.

Open Scallop Hat

Approximately 2" in diameter, 1" high

Materials:

DMC Cebelia #10, 9 yds.
Size 7 steel crochet hook
1 ft. ¼"-wide ribbon
Sewing thread

Ch 5; join with sl st in first ch to form ring.

Rnd 1: Ch 1, 10 sc in ring; join in first sc.

Rnd 2: Ch 5 (counts as dc and ch 2), (dc in next sc, ch 2) 9 times, sl st in 3rd ch of beg ch 5.

Rnds 3–4: Ch 5, (dc in next dc, ch 2) 9 times, sl st in 3rd ch of beg ch 5.

Rnds 5–6: Ch 6 (counts as dc and ch 3), (dc in next dc, ch 3) 9 times, sl st in 3rd ch of beg ch 6.

Rnd 7: Ch 1, work sc, hdc, dc, hdc, and sc in each ch-3 sp around; join in first sc.

Rnd 8: Work sl st and ch 1 in each st around; join in first sl st and fasten off.

Starch the hat. Make a ribbon bow and sew it to the hat.

Stocking

Approximately 2¾" long

Materials:

DMC Cebelia #10, 14 yds.
Size 7 steel crochet hook
1 ft. ½"-wide ribbon

Foot: Ch 4, join with sl st in first ch to form ring.

Rnd 1: Ch 1, 8 sc in ring; join in first sc.

Rnd 2: Ch 1, 2 sc in same sp, 2 sc in each sc around; join in first sc—16 sc.

Rnds 3–4: Ch 1, sc in same sp, sc in each sc around.

Rnd 5: Ch 4 (counts as dc and ch 1), (skip next sc, dc in next sc, ch 1) 7 times, join with sl st in 3rd ch of beg ch 4.

Rnds 6-7: Ch 4, (dc in next dc, ch 1) 7 times, join with sl st in 3rd ch of beg ch 4.

Heel—Row 1: Ch 1, turn; sc in same sp, sc in next ch-1 sp, (sc in next dc, sc in next ch-1 sp) 3 times—8 sc.

Row 2: Ch 1, turn; sc in each of 8 sc.

Row 3: Ch 1, turn; skip first sc, sc in each of next 6 sc.

Row 4: Ch 1, turn; sc in each of 6 sc.

Row 5: Ch 1, turn; skip first sc, sc in each of next 4 sc.

Row 6: Ch 1, turn; sc in each of 4 sc.

(continued on the next page)

Row 7: Ch 1, turn; skip first sc, sc in each of next 2 sc.

Row 8: Ch 1, turn; sc in each of 2 sc.

Leg—Rnd 8: Ch 4 (right side), (dc in end of next row, ch 1, skip next row) 4 times, (dc in next dc, ch 1) 4 times, (dc in end of next row, ch 1, skip next row) 4 times; join in 3rd ch of beg ch 4.

Rnds 9–16: Ch 4, (dc in next dc, ch 1) 12 times, join in 3rd ch of beg ch 4.

Rnd 17: *Sc in next dc, sc in next ch-1 sp; rep from * around; join.

Rnd 18: Work sl st and ch 1 in each st around; join and fasten off.

Starch the stocking. Make a ribbon bow and attach it to the top of the stocking.

Spidery Snowflake

Approximately 3¼" in diameter

Materials:

DMC Cebelia #30, 8 yds.
Size 12 steel crochet hook

Ch 16; join with sl st in first ch to form ring.

Rnd 1: Ch 2 (counts as hdc), 29 hdc in ring; sl st in top of beg ch 2.

Rnd 2: Ch 1, sc in same sp, ch 25, skip next 4 hdc, (sc in next hdc, ch 25, skip next 4 hdc) 5 times. Fasten off.

Rnd 3: Join to top of any ch-25 lp, ch 1, sc in same lp, *(ch 9, sl st in 9th ch from hook for picot) 3 times, sc in same ch-25 lp, ch 9, work 3 p, sl st in base of first p of group, ch 9,** sc in next ch-25 lp; rep from * 4 times; rep from * to ** once; sl st in first sc of rnd. Fasten off.

Open Star

Approximately 4" in diameter

Materials:

DMC Cebelia #10, 9 yds.
Size 7 steel crochet hook

Ch 6; join with sl st in first ch to form ring.

Rnd 1: Ch 1, 15 sc in ring; join in first sc.

Rnd 2: Ch 1, sc and hdc in same sp, 2 dc in next sc, hdc and sc in next sc, (sc and hdc in next sc, 2 dc in next sc, hdc and sc in next sc) 4 times; join in first sc—5 points.

Rnd 3: Ch 13, (skip point, sc in sp bet points, ch 12) 4 times, join in first ch of beg ch 13.

Rnd 4: Sl st in each of next 6 chs, (ch 20, sl st in next ch-12 lp) 5 times; join at base of first ch 20.

Rnd 5: Ch 1, (work 11 sc in ch-20 lp, ch 4, sl st in first ch of ch 4 for picot, ch 5, sl st in first ch of ch 5 for picot, ch 4, sl st in first ch of ch 4 for picot, sl st in sl st of first picot, work 11 sc in remainder of ch-20 lp, sl st bet lps) 5 times; join and fasten off.

Ruffled Popcorn Wreath

Approximately 3½" in diameter

Materials:

DMC Cebelia #10, 23 yds.
Size 7 steel crochet hook

½ yd. ⅜"-wide ribbon
Sewing thread

Beginning Popcorn (BPC): Ch 4, *yo twice, insert hook in same sp, draw up a lp, (yo and pull through 2 lps on hook) twice*, rep bet *s twice more in same sp, yo and pull through all 4 lps on hook, ch 1.

Popcorn (PC): *Yo twice, insert hook in st and draw up a lp, (yo and pull through 2 lps on hook) twice*; rep bet *s 3 times in same sp, yo, pull through all 5 lps on hook, ch 1.

Ch 30; join with sl st in first ch to form ring, being very careful not to twist chain.

Rnd 1: Ch 2 (counts as hdc), 2 hdc in next ch, (hdc in next ch, 2 hdc in next ch) 13 times, hdc in each of last 2 ch; join in top of beg ch 2—44 hdc.

Rnd 2: Work BPC, ch 1, *skip next st, work PC and ch 1 in next st; rep from * around; join in top of BPC.

Rnd 3: Sl st to first ch-sp bet PCs, ch 5 (counts as dc and ch 2), (dc in same ch-sp, ch 2) twice, work (dc and ch 2) 3 times in each ch-sp; join in 3rd ch of ch 5.

Rnd 4: Sl st to first ch-2 sp, work (sc and ch 2) twice in each ch-2 sp around. Join and fasten off.

Starch the wreath. Make a ribbon bow with long streamers and tack it to the wreath.

Lacy Round Star

Approximately 2½" in diameter

Materials:

DMC Cebelia #30, 8 yds.
Size 12 steel crochet hook

Ch 10; join with sl st in first ch to form ring.

Rnd 1: Ch 1, 2 sc in each ch of ring; sl st in first sc of rnd—20 sc.

Rnd 2: Ch 1, sc in same sp, ch 6, (sc in next sc, ch 6) 18 times, ch 3, dc in first sc of rnd (this brings thread into position for next rnd).

Rnd 3: Ch 1, sc around post of dc just made, ch 12, (sc in next ch-6 lp, ch 12) 18 times; ch 5, yo hook 4 times, draw up a lp in first sc of rnd, (yo and draw through 2 lps) 5 times.

Rnd 4: Ch 1, sc around post of st just made, (*ch 9, sl st in 9th ch from hook for picot*) 3 times, sc in same sp, *(ch 3, sc in next ch-12 lp) 3 times, ch 3* sc in next ch-12 lp, work 3 p, sc in same lp; rep from * 3 times; rep bet *s once; sl st in first sc of rnd. Fasten off.

Blocking Guides

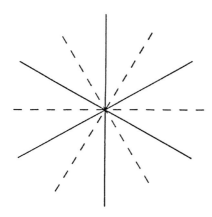

6- or 12-pointed
Snowflakes

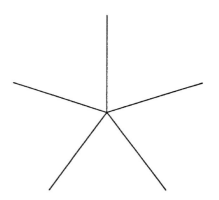

Star

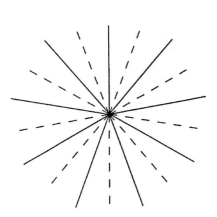

9- or 18-pointed
Ornaments

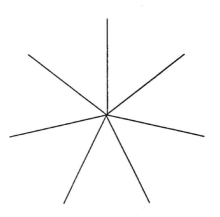

7-pointed
Ornaments

Slip Knot

Grasp the loose end of the thread with your left hand and make an "O" with the thread leading from the ball (the ball of thread should be hanging behind the "O"). Pinch the top of the "O" between the thumb and middle finger of your left hand, and hold your crochet hook in your right hand as you would hold a pencil. Insert the tip of the hook and bring a loop from the thread ball through the "O" (*Fig. 1*). Tighten the loop to complete the slip knot (*Fig. 2*). You are now ready to make your first chain stitch (remember that the loop on your hook never counts when you are counting the stitches in your work).

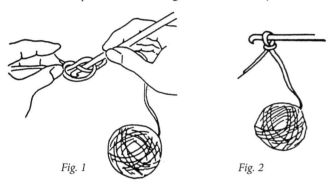

Fig. 1   *Fig. 2*

Chain Stitch

Pinch the base of the slip knot between the thumb and middle finger of your left hand, and wind the thread from the ball from back to front over your forefinger. With the crochet hook inserted in the slip knot and the tip of the hook curved toward you, wrap the thread around the hook from back to front (*Fig. 3*)—this is called a yarn over. Pull the thread through the loop on the hook to complete the first chain stitch. Yarn over again and pull through the loop on the hook the number of times specified (*Fig. 4*). Each chain (and later each single crochet or other stitch) forms a distinct oval that can be clearly seen from the top of the work.

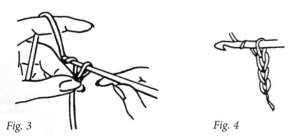

Fig. 3   *Fig. 4*

Counting the Chain Stitches: Just as a slip knot must be placed on the hook in the beginning, there must always be a loop on the hook before starting a new stitch. The loop on the hook is considered the beginning of each

succeeding stitch and, therefore, does not count as a stitch. In a row of chain stitches, the chain stitch next to the loop on the hook is counted as the first stitch from the hook, the chain stitch preceding that one is the second stitch from the hook, and so on (*Fig. 5*).

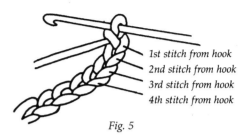

1st stitch from hook
2nd stitch from hook
3rd stitch from hook
4th stitch from hook

Fig. 5

Single Crochet

Make a foundation chain of the required number of stitches (remember that the loop on the hook does not count as a stitch and that, for single crochet, you will need one chain for each stitch you want to make plus one additional chain for turning). Keeping the thread from the ball wrapped from back to front over your left forefinger, begin the first single crochet stitch by inserting the hook from front to back in the second chain from the hook, taking care to push the hook through the center of the oval (*Fig. 6*). Then yarn over—that is, bring the thread over the hook from back to front (*Fig. 7*)—and pull the thread through the stitch. You now have two loops on the hook (*Fig. 8*). Yarn over again (*Fig. 9*) and pull the thread through both loops on the hook to complete the first single crochet stitch (*Fig. 10*). You now have only one loop left on the hook and are ready to begin the

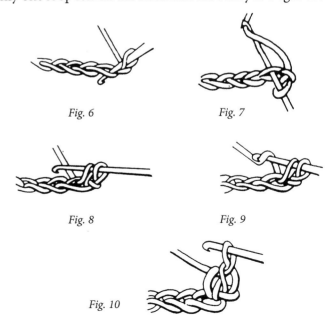

Fig. 6   *Fig. 7*

Fig. 8   *Fig. 9*

Fig. 10

next stitch. Repeat the procedure until you have worked one single crochet stitch in each stitch of the foundation chain. Unless the pattern instructions specify otherwise, begin your next row of single crochet by making one chain stitch. Make your first stitch in the second stitch from the hook, inserting the hook under both strands that form the oval of the stitch of the previous row.

Half Double Crochet

Make a foundation chain of the required number of stitches (remember that the loop on the hook does not count as a stitch and that, for hdc, you will need one chain for each stitch you want to make plus two additional chains for turning). To begin the first half double crochet stitch, first make sure that the thread from the ball is wrapped from back to front over your left forefinger. Then yarn over (bring the thread over the hook from back to front) (*Fig. 11*) and insert the hook from front to back in the third chain from the hook, taking care to push the hook through the center of the oval. Yarn over again and pull the thread through the stitch. You now have three loops on the hook (*Fig. 12*). Yarn over once more and pull the thread through all three loops on the hook to complete the first half double crochet stitch (*Fig. 13*). You now have only one loop left on the hook and are ready to begin the next stitch. Repeat the procedure until you have worked one half double crochet stitch in each stitch of the foundation chain. Unless the pattern instructions specify otherwise, begin your next row of half double crochet by making two chain stitches. Make your next stitch in the third stitch from the hook, inserting the hook under both strands that form the oval of the stitch of the previous row. The two chain stitches will count as your first half double crochet stitch.

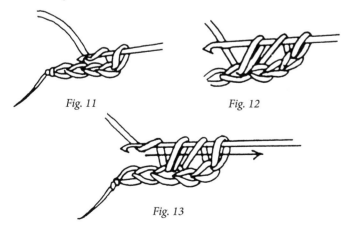

Fig. 11   Fig. 12

Fig. 13

Double Crochet

Make a foundation chain of the required number of stitches (remember that the loop on the hook does not count as a stitch and that, for double crochet, you will need one chain for each stitch you want to make plus three

additional chains for turning). To begin the first double crochet stitch, first make sure that the thread from the ball is wrapped from back to front over your left forefinger. Then yarn over (bring the thread over the hook from back to front) (*Fig. 14*) and insert the hook from front to back in the fourth chain from the hook, taking care to push the hook through the center of the oval. Yarn over again and pull the thread through the stitch. You now have three loops on the hook (*Fig. 15*). Yarn over again and pull the thread through the first two loops on the hook. You now have two loops left on the hook. Yarn over once more (*Fig. 16*) and pull the thread through both of the loops on the hook to complete the first double crochet stitch (*Fig. 17*). You now have only one loop left on the hook and are ready to begin the next stitch. Repeat the procedure until you have worked one double crochet stitch in each stitch of the foundation chain. Unless the pattern instructions specify otherwise, begin your next row of double crochet by making three chain stitches. Make your next stitch in the fourth stitch from the hook, inserting the hook under both strands that form the oval of the stitch of the previous row. The three chain stitches will count as your first double crochet stitch.

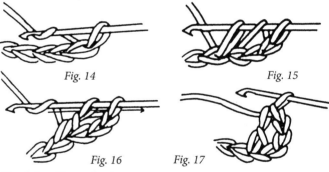

Fig. 14   Fig. 15

Fig. 16   Fig. 17

Treble Crochet

Make a foundation chain of the required number of stitches (remember that the loop on the hook does not count as a stitch and that, for treble crochet, you will need one chain for each stitch you want to make plus four additional chains for turning). To begin the first treble crochet stitch, first make sure that the thread from the ball is wrapped from back to front over your left forefinger. Then yarn over (bring the thread over the hook from back to front) twice (*Fig. 18*) and insert the hook from front to back in the fifth chain from the hook, taking care to push the hook through the center of the oval. Yarn over again and pull the thread through the stitch. You now have four loops on the hook (*Fig. 19*). Yarn over again and pull the

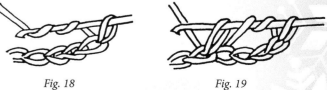

Fig. 18   Fig. 19

thread through the first two loops on the hook. You now have three loops left on the hook. Yarn over once more and pull the thread through the next two loops on the hook. You now have two loops left on the hook. Yarn over once more and pull the thread through both of the loops on the hook to complete the first treble crochet stitch. You now have only one loop left on the hook and are ready to begin the next stitch. Repeat the procedure until you have worked one treble crochet stitch in each stitch of the foundation chain. Unless the pattern instructions specify otherwise, begin your next row of treble crochet by making four chain stitches. Make your next stitch in the fifth stitch from the hook, inserting the hook under both strands that form the oval of the stitch of the previous row. The four chain stitches will count as your first treble crochet stitch.

Double Treble Crochet

Make a foundation chain of the required number of stitches (remember that the loop on the hook does not count as a stitch and that, for double treble crochet, you will need one chain for each stitch you want to make plus five additional chains for turning). To begin the first double treble crochet stitch, first make sure that the thread from the ball is wrapped from back to front over your left forefinger. Then yarn over (bring the thread over the hook from back to front) three times (*Fig. 20*)

Fig. 20

and insert the hook from front to back in the sixth chain from the hook, taking care to push the hook through the center of the oval. Yarn over again and pull the thread through the stitch. You now have five loops on the hook. Yarn over again and pull the thread through the first two loops on the hook. You now have four loops left on the hook. Yarn over again and pull the thread through the next two loops on the hook. You now have three loops left on the hook. Yarn over once more and pull the thread through the next two loops on the hook. You now have two loops left on the hook. Yarn over once more and pull the thread through both of the loops on the hook to complete the first double treble crochet stitch. You now have only one loop left on the hook and are ready to begin the next stitch. Repeat the procedure until you have worked one double treble crochet stitch in each stitch of the foundation chain. Unless the pattern instructions specify otherwise, begin your next row of treble crochet by making five chain stitches. Make your next stitch in

the sixth stitch from the hook, inserting the hook under both strands that form the oval of the stitch of the previous row. The five chain stitches will count as your first treble crochet stitch.

Slip Stitch

Insert the hook in a stitch, yarn over and then pull the thread through both the stitch and the loop on the hook in one motion (*Fig. 21*). Slip stitch is similar to single crochet, but you do not yarn over a second time before pulling the thread through the loop on the hook.

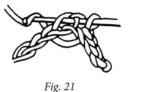

Fig. 21

Fig. 22

Working in Rounds

In many of these ornaments, you will be working in "rounds." To do this, first join the ends of the beginning chain with a slip stitch to form a ring (*Fig. 22*). For the first "round," work the required number of stitches either in the chain stitches or in the ring itself. In most cases, you will end each round by working a slip stitch in the first stitch of the round. Because you are working around in a circle, you will not have to turn the work after each round and will always be working on the same side of the work. Each new round will begin with one or more chains to bring your hook into position for the next stitch. With the exception of single crochet, this beginning chain will count as one of the stitches in the round. It is a good idea to mark the beginning stitch of each round with a safety pin or paper clip, since it can be difficult to find the beginning otherwise.

Working in the Back Loops

When a ribbed effect is desired, the pattern instructions will tell you to work one or more rows or rounds in the back loops only. This means that, instead of inserting the hook in the customary way under both strands that form the oval of the stitch of the previous row or round, you must insert the hook under only the back strand (the one furthest from you) of the stitch (*Fig. 23*).

Fig. 23

Working in the Front Loops

The pattern instructions will sometimes tell you to work one or more rows or rounds in the *front* loops only. This means that, instead of inserting the hook under both strands that form the oval of the stitch of the previous row or round, you must insert the hook under only the front strand (the one closest to you) of the stitch.

Working in a Chain Space

A series of chain stitches is often used to bridge an open space—as, for example, when working a lace-like design. To crochet the next row or round, the pattern instructions may tell you to work across the "bridge" of chain stitches by working in the chain space rather than into the chain stitches themselves. This means that, to make each of the stitches in question, you must insert the hook into the space under the chain (*Fig. 24*) and then work the stitch around the chain (*Fig. 25*).

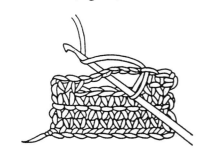

Fig. 24

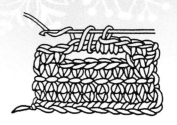

Fig. 25

Increasing and Decreasing

To increase one stitch, work two stitches in the same stitch of the previous row. To decrease one stitch, either skip a stitch of the previous row or work two stitches together as follows: work the first stitch until the final yarn over, but do not yarn over; instead, begin to work the next stitch, working it also to the final yarn over; now yarn over and pull the thread through all loops on the hook.

Ending Off

Complete the last stitch of the piece and cut the thread from the ball, leaving a 4" thread end (or a thread end of the length specified in the instructions). Then draw the thread end through the remaining loop on the hook and pull tight. Thread the thread end onto a large-eyed needle and weave it through the back of the work for about 1". Trim the excess.

Abbreviations

beg	begin or beginning		prev	previous
bet	between		rem	remaining
ch(s)	chain(s)		rep	repeat
ch-sp	chain space		rnd(s)	round(s)
dc	double crochet		sc	single crochet
dec	decrease		sl st(s)	slip stitch(es)
dtr	double treble crochet		sp(s)	space(s)
ft	foot/feet		st(s)	stitch(es)
hdc	half double crochet		tr	treble crochet
inc	increase		yd(s)	yard(s)
lp(s)	loop(s)		yo	yarn over
p	picot			

The terminology and hooks listed in this book are those used in the United States. The following charts give the U.S. names of crochet stitches and their equivalents in other countries and the approximate equivalents to U.S. crochet hook sizes.

Stitch Conversion Chart

U.S. Name	Equivalent
Chain	Chain
Slip	Single crochet
Single crochet	Double crochet
Half-double or short-double crochet	Half-treble crochet
Double crochet	Treble crochet
Treble crochet	Double-treble crochet
Double-treble crochet	Treble-treble crochet
Treble-treble or long-treble crochet	Quadruple-treble crochet
Afghan stitch	Tricot crochet

Steel Crochet Hook Conversion Chart

U.S. Size	00	0	1	2	3	4	5	6	7	8	9	10	11	12	13	14
British & Canadian Size	000	00	0	1	–	1½	2	2½	–	3	–	4	–	5	–	6
Metric Size (mm)	3.00	2.75	2.50	2.25	2.10	2.00	1.90	1.80	1.65	1.50	1.40	1.25	1.10	1.00	0.75	0.60